Ladies of the Lamplight

by Kay Reynolds Blair

WESTERN REFLECTIONS

PUBLISHING COMPANY

Revised Edition

ISBN 1-890437-41-7

Library of Congress Catalog Number: 00-102174

Cover and text by SJS Design, Susan Smilanic

Western Reflections Publishing Company
P.O. Box 710
Ouray, Colorado 81427
U.S.A.

For Darrell and Kimery. And for Ned.

Table of Contents

Inside a bagnio. Courtesy: Denver Public Library Western Collection.

Some Facts About The Fancies

Women who strayed from the accepted norm of behavior found themselves outcasts from respectable society. And it was easy to fall from the accepted pattern - there was not much leeway given and there were very few occupations a woman could enter to support herself. Any woman who did not adhere to society's rigid standard of behavior was scorned and labeled "fast," "easy," or a "fallen woman." Certainly, women who were kept, or were mistresses, were ostracized. Yet men who kept women, who were womanizers, and who frequented cribs, dance halls and parlor houses, were accepted by their peers and continued their lives as usual. Their wives often overlooked such behavior as long as the men were discreet. Many women who lost their respectable reputations found their way to being dance hall girls, prostitutes, madams and a few became gamblers, robbers and rustlers.

There was a wide range of "fallen women." Even within their outcast status, there was a hierarchy. The lowest on the ladder were the girls who worked in the cribs. The cribs were a series of rooms, wide enough for a door and one to two windows across the front and long enough to hold a bed, a stove and a dresser with a wash basin. Some were eight feet wide and ten to twelve feet long. There might be some photos and pictures of pastoral scenes on the walls. Larger cribs might have a small front parlor and a small bedroom behind it. These units generally rented for $25 a week and the girls who used them sold themselves for twenty-five cents to a dollar fifty. According to a Texas Bluebook of 1911, a Class A girl ($1.50) usually weighed 160 to 200 pounds. They might also sell beer to their customers and add a bit to the price for some extra money. The women would stand outside their doors and solicit men coming by until many towns passed ordinances prohibiting such practices. Then they moved inside and would stand at the window and in some places, where the curtains were required to be drawn, they would punch holes in the curtains so potential customers could take a peek at the merchandise.

The next level encompassed the dance hall girls, saloon girls and girls in the theaters. Society looked upon these women less harshly, since not all were selling their favors. Dance hall girls were generally well dressed, some wearing costumes costing as much as $700. Men would buy a ticket for one dollar to dance with the girl and very popular ones might earn enough in tips and wages to avoid selling sex. Saloon girls pushed drinks and served drinks and received a commission on what they sold. Their outfits usually consisted of a low-cut bodice, short skirt and silk stockings. They, too, had the option of selling their favors or not. The theater girls performed on stage - singing, dancing and pushing drinks which added a commission to their performance wage. They also could "work the boxes" if they chose and sell themselves to the men who invited them into their box seats on the second floor. These establishments usually had a back or side entrance for men who wanted a box at the theater but didn't want to be seen entering or leaving the establishment.

The highest ranking girls were those in the best houses of prostitution. The houses themselves depended on the madam and what clientele she would accept. Naturally, the first class houses would charge more. The madam of any house had to be a good businesswoman and keep her girls in line, keep her clientele in line, avoid being cheated, be charming when necessary and strict when necessary. She might have a bouncer, a bartender, a cook, and a piano player working for her as well as her girls.

There was a variety of arrangements between madams and their boarders. Some were given room, board and a clothing allowance and received one fourth or more of their earnings plus any tips. Other girls would pay for room and/or board and buy their own clothing and receive half their earnings plus tips. Some received a commission on drinks they sold. Others were paid weekly wages ranging from $30 to $60. Some madams charged the boarders $20 to $40 a week and then allowed any excess money to be kept by the girls. A system of brass checks was instituted by many madams to avoid cheating. The customer purchased the brass check or token and gave it to the girl, who in turn gave it to the madam to collect her pay. In the Denver area, women were purchased for $5 for a quick date and up to $30 for the entire night. The houses were open from noon to dawn and usually had ten to twenty girls working there. Usually there were two meals served, a late breakfast before opening at noon, and supper around 5 p.m. Each girl had one day off a week. The girls in the parlor houses never associated with the women in the cribs. They had to appear to be a more exclusive commodity.

The madams and some prostitutes had poodles for pets and would take them out walking. A Denver fire chief wrecked the department's first automobile when he tried to avoid one of the white poodles on Market Street. There were so many who owned these dogs that no respectable lady would dare own one.

The madams were not all business. Nell Kimball, a madam from New Orleans, wrote in her book, *Nell Kimball, Her Life as an American Madame by Herself*, "I got into the habit of going out to Colorado - the fine thin air was grand after the humid stuff in the Gulf. A lot of the madams would do the same and we'd meet and dine and talk shop in Denver at the old Windsor - all mirrors and ormolu and fine plush, like any high class cat house, or we'd hire a fancy rig and go down to Louie Dupuy's Hotel de Paris in Georgetown, the Teller House in Central City, Haw Tabor's Vendome Hotel in Leadville."

The term "Red Light District" originated with railroad men carrying their red lamps and leaving them outside the doors of cribs. Later, it was commonly accepted as meaning any area of prostitution, whether cribs or parlor houses.

Prostitution served a need in the rough, raw camps, whether they were cattle towns or mining towns or railroad hubs. And it flourished until respectable ladies and children moved in and settled the area and brought their opinions and way of life to the communities. With increased civilization in the towns, new laws were passed to rid the communities of undesirable elements and behavior. Thus legal prostitution was outlawed and the trade decreased.

The women themselves, from the lowest rung to the top, met a variety of ends. Some were lucky and married out of the trade, others committed suicide or succumbed to venereal disease or died of complications from an abortion or were murdered by a jealous man or a rival prostitute. Others died young from drug abuse or natural causes, hastened by a hard life.

Brass checks were used for trade instead of money. Photo: Author's collection.

Buckskin Joe, a neighboring community to Dudley. Courtesy: State Historical Society of Colorado Library.

Silver Heels

The story of Silver Heels unfolded in the Fairplay area. According to old timers she was a dance hall girl in Buckskin Joe, a small mining town some seven miles from Fairplay. The town started in 1861 and was deserted by 1864. During its brief but flashy existence it was the county seat of Park County, had a court house, a theater, dance halls, a post office, saloons, parlor houses, two banks, respectable businesses and even a brass band. H.A.W. Tabor set up shop there before he ventured to Oro City (which later became Leadville).

Silver Heels may have been a dance-hall girl or she may have worked at one of the parlor houses. She was described as "beautiful of face" and could dance faster and more gracefully than anyone. She wore glittering silver slippers that gave rise to her nickname. Her good nature was well known and she became the idol of the camp. Shortly after her arrival, she fell in love with one of the miners and they were engaged to be married.

Tragedy struck Buckskin Joe in the form of a smallpox epidemic. The town closed down. Women retreated to Fairplay to escape exposure. But Silver Heels stayed and nursed her lover who had contracted the dread disease. He was one of the first to die. After his death Silver Heels stayed on and nursed the infected miners and their families. She kept house for the sick, cooked their meals, washed their clothes, and helped them through the worst of the disease.

When the epidemic broke and the town showed signs of life again, the grateful living collected a fund of money to give to Silver Heels in appreciation of her deeds. She could not be found. She had left Buckskin Joe without a word. The miners wanted to do something for her and they decided to name the highest and most beautiful mountain in the district after the girl who gave so much to them.

Several years later, a woman draped in heavy black veils visited the cemetery beneath Mt. Silver Heels and the miners believed it was indeed the Silver Heels of the past, returning to walk near her lover's grave. So ends a legend.

Albert B. Sanford has presented another story of Silver Heels in a paper entitled "Silver Heels." This account was told to him by Tom Lee who had lived in the camp where "Silver Heels" appeared, and though not as romantic as the legend, is probably closer to the truth.

The story took place in a small town, possibly Dudley, although Tom Lee does not give the name of the town. Dudley was a small town, and most important, had a mill that handled the ore from the Moose Mine. Tom Lee's account put the town near Buckskin Joe, Montgomery, Alma and Fairplay and the hero of the story had a mill. This version of Silver Heels' story also puts the date in the early 1870s.

A young woman arrived in the camp one day on the Denver stage. The usual crowd had gathered to wait for mail and news and they noticed she seemed "lost and confused."

Jack Herndon, owner of the main saloon and gambling hall, was with the group and she asked his assistance with her baggage and if he would show her to the hotel.

Jack took her to Mr. and Mrs. Mack's house, as they had the cleanest and best house in town. After reaching the residence the girl fainted and was taken to a room next to Mrs. Mack's where the kindly woman nursed her. She told Mrs. Mack her story, which Mrs.

Mack never divulged and from that time on they were like mother and daughter.

The townsfolk knew about the fainting incident and asked Jack who the girl was. He took a lot of kidding about his helping her and everyone thought he must know her. He didn't. But he soon found her name was Josie Dillon. He also found that she had asked about him and had been disappointed when she discovered he ran the saloon and gambling hall.

Josie helped the Macks in the kitchen when business was crowded and also became a favorite of the children in town. She sent to Denver for candy and would have the children visit in the afternoons and tell them stories and recite verses for them.

Life went along as usual in the small town until autumn. Then word came of the great Chicago fire (October 8, 1871). Communities throughout the country were shocked by the devastation of the fire and the plight of the homeless. Meetings were organized to raise money for the victims of the fire and to gather food and clothing to be sent to help the needy.

Jack Herndon responded to the call in his community. He closed his bar, had benches built and organized a meeting to discuss what the citizens could do to help the Chicago people. Several ideas were discussed and the people finally decided an entertainment program to raise money would be the best thing, but no one agreed on what would be on the program. Mr. and Mrs. Mack and Josie came to the meeting late and after listening to the various ideas, Josie asked if she could help. She thought the entertainment program would be nice and she offered to help with the program saying she could do some dancing and singing. She explained she had been on stage at one time, and that came as a shock to everyone. Her request was that instead of passing the hat to collect money or charging admission, they should set up a box and let the people donate whatever they wished.

The people applauded enthusiastically and Josie's idea was the one decided upon. They scheduled the program for two nights later and Jack said his business would be closed till after the show so they could get ready. Mr. and Mrs. Mack said they would donate coffee and cakes to take care of the crowd. The meeting broke up and everyone was busy starting their plans, including Jack, Josie, and Mr. and Mrs. Mack.

The next afternoon Josie got together with a lady who played piano and, luckily, Jack had a piano at his gambling hall. Also at the rehearsal were two or three good fiddlers and a Negro boy who played guitar. No one knew what the program would be except those who were providing it.

Help came from the neighboring communities; men came over to build more benches to sit on and a platform at one end of the hall to be the stage.

The big night arrived, the crowd came, and the house was full. Jack opened the meeting with the latest news from Chicago and explained the box up front was for donations when the show was over. He turned the meeting over to Johnny Dyer, a young lawyer in the camp who had lived in Chicago. Johnny told the people where the fire had started, what it had destroyed, portrayed the plight of the victims and told them every bit collected that night would go to Chicago immediately.

Josie was introduced then, and she gave a little speech about the people in the community, how they believed in giving others a hand, and told how she had studied for the stage. She said she would sing some songs and do some dances and she hoped she would please them. The band played a little music while Josie changed for her first number and then Johnny Dyer announced Josie and her accompanist.

"Well, if the moon had dropped out of the sky it wouldn't have given the crowd a greater surprise. Josie came out in a dress a bit short but modest and it glittered with what most of the fellows thought was diamonds riveted in bands around her throat and on the edge of her dress. But her slippers! Silver all over except the toes and they were gold."

Josie performed a Spanish dance, an Irish jig, and a Highland fling. Then the band entertained while Josie changed to a long dress and powdered wig to do her next number, a dance of Washington's time. The band played again and Josie changed to her regular clothes, but she kept her silver slippers on through the whole performance. This time she sang "Old Home Down on the Farm" to conclude the program. The audience begged for one more song, so Josie accommodated them with "Home, Sweet Home." She sang it so sweetly that "there were some of those old bearded geezers with tears in their eyes as big as hazel nuts."

The line passed the collection box, dropping greenbacks in the box and gold dust in a stone crock. The audience had given seventeen hundred and fifty dollars, which was more than the other camps had raised combined. The group finished up the evening eating doughnuts and cakes and drinking coffee, all provided by Mr. and Mrs. Mack. It had been an evening the little camp would remember for years to come.

After the money-raising project, the camp settled down again and business resumed as usual. But Jack didn't seem to take as much interest in his gambling hall and saloon and he soon told Tom Lee that he was going to Denver to try to sell the place and he wanted Lee to build him a cabin up in one of the gulches.

Jack returned from Denver, followed shortly by two men who spent a lot of time in the saloon and gambling hall, looking the place over. A deal was made, Jack sold the hall to the men and they closed the agreement in the cabin Tom had built.

Jack went into mining a claim of his own, did well, and built a mill that was prospering too. He and Josie were seeing each other and things seemed to be moving along fine. About that time some Mexicans brought in sheep from the San Luis Valley to butcher for market and two of the men came down with smallpox. The Mexicans didn't let anyone know about the situation and when it was discovered there was talk of hanging them.

The sheepherders were the first to die of the disease and members of the town who had had smallpox started nursing the sick. Jack, Josie, and Mr. and Mrs. Mack jumped in to organize the situation and soon Jack took ill, though not seriously. Josie and the Macks nursed him back to health. Josie sent to Denver for two doctors and some nurses, although Tom Lee was the only one who knew she did it. They were brought in on the stage and Josie arranged for the gambling hall, which had a dance hall added to it under the new management, to be used as a hospital. The hall, as well as other businesses, had closed down when the epidemic hit. Word was sent from the Wells Fargo office in Denver that all bills for doctors and nurses from Denver would be paid by the Wells Fargo office in Fairplay when presented there. Josie had arranged to pay the bills through Wells Fargo so the miners wouldn't know she did it.

Josie worked all through the epidemic, nursing the sick from early morning to late at night. The patients had good care from Josie, the nurses and doctors, and there were only a few deaths. Josie, luckily, did not contract the disease.

During the time of the epidemic the miners remembered Josie's performance and began calling her Silver Heels. Jack wasn't happy about that, but Josie told him they meant no harm and always addressed her personally as "Miss Josie." So her nickname began and Silver Heels took a place in the miners' hearts.

Shortly after the epidemic Josie left for Denver and Jack followed a week later. Everyone knew they were in love and suspected they planned to get married. They were married and returned to the camp on a special coach. The town gave them a reception to be remembered. Josie and Jack had a new home built and they lived there a year or so. They had a baby daughter during this time and named her Marion Lee Herndon. Jack passed around cigars and the townspeople rejoiced with the happy couple. Josie's parents visited the couple and their new granddaughter but not long after Jack got word his father had died. His mother wanted them to come and live with her in Kentucky.

It was a hard decision for them to make because they loved the camp and the people. But they decided they must go. Jack and Josie left their house and land to Tom Lee because of his friendship to them. The townspeople gathered to see them off. Josie spoke to the crowd before the stage departed, saying, "I have learned to love this place and its people. None of you can understand how much I regret leaving, but it seems for the best. I'll never forget you and shall always feel that you care for Jack and I and our little Marion Lee Herndon." The couple rode off, leaving a sad group behind.

Sometime after the Herndons had departed a survey crew came through mapping the area and needed a name for one of the big mountains. They asked the miners to have a meeting and choose a name. The name Silver Heels was suggested and, no doubt, Tom Lee was the one to do it. The vote for his choice was unanimous. Silver Heels would always be remembered in the country she loved so well.

Cabin in California Gulch. Courtesy: State Historical Society of Colorado Library

Red Stockings

    The story of Red Stockings is one of the shortest, and perhaps one of the happiest of the tales of Colorado's "ladies of the lamplight." At least for many girls of the bordellos and dance halls, Red Stockings had the love they envied.

    California Gulch (the forerunner of Leadville) was opened up by Abe Lee in April 1860. Lee discovered gold there, the news spread and by that summer 5,000 people had flocked to the gulch. A small town grew up around the one street and every imaginable form of crude building was used to house the new arrivals. Log cabins, tents, wagons, bough houses, and dugouts nestled in the tree-filled area. Game was plentiful and several hundred placer claims proved plentiful also.

    Red Stockings was one of the hordes that swarmed to the gold diggings and most likely she was one of the first ladies of pleasure in the settlement. Red Stockings was described as young, a small woman with flashing black eyes and a brilliant smile. She wore red ribbons in her hair and, in keeping with her name, red stockings. She was said to have been cultured and refined, the daughter of a Boston merchant. Her past included a French nobleman and a New York gambler, who had been temporary husbands. While in California Gulch she ruled like a queen.

The first winter found the camp deserted. Some went to the Gunnison country to trap beaver; others went to Denver. They were not prepared with enough supplies to spend the winter, but with the return of spring the miners once more filled the gulch.

At the close of 1861 Red Stockings gave a banquet for some of the men of the camp and told them she had made enough money and had had enough good times. She was going to be respectable. Reportedly, Red Stockings had made $100,000 during her short stay. She married, moved to Nevada, and had a family. She carried out the dream that many of her type had - to make their money fast, get married, and be accepted by society.

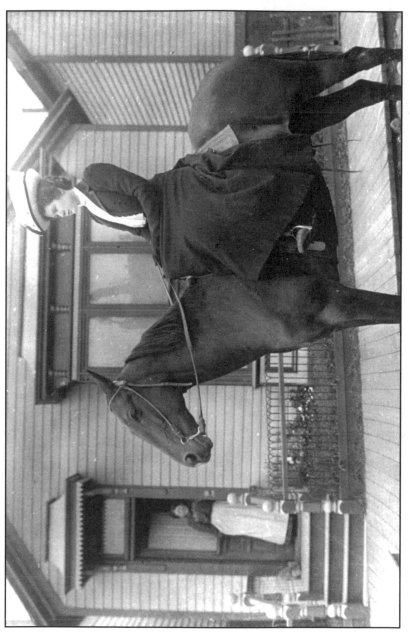

A respectable lady out for a ride. The "dream ambition" of many prostitutes was to become respectable. Photo: Author's collection.

Poker Alice in her seventies. Courtesy: Denver Public Library Western Collection.

Poker Alice

Alice Ivers began her career as a master gambler in Lake City, Colorado. Her background did not indicate her future career in any manner. Alice was born in England, the daughter of a respected schoolteacher. Her parents moved to America and she was educated in the South in a girls' school. No doubt her upbringing and education trained her to be a lady and her life in the gambling halls of boomtowns was a far cry from her intended way of life.

Alice married a mining engineer, Frank Duffield, and they moved to Lake City. It was in this rough mining town that she began playing cards. Her husband would take her to the gambling halls for entertainment where she would watch the games in fascination. She learned how to play and then began playing for fun. Alice was lucky and good at cards. Then Frank was killed in a mining accident and Alice was left to support herself. There were no schools in Lake City where she could teach, but there were plenty of gambling dens. So she began her career as a professional gambler.

When Lake City began to close up for the winter months, Alice would move to other towns in the district along with the miners and other gamblers. She played cards - faro and stud poker her favorites - in the district for several years, and then began her wanderings to newer surroundings. While in New Mexico, she played against one of the gambling houses until she broke the bank. When the dealer closed the game, Alice took over, banking it herself and putting no limit on the bets. She played through the night against all comers and made several thousand dollars. She took her winnings, went to New York City, had a fling and then returned to the mining camps to play again.

Alice saw the people and places of much of the West. She gambled in Colorado, New Mexico, Arizona, Oklahoma, Kansas, Texas and South Dakota. She was one of the first to arrive at Creede, Colorado, and she had to cut logs for her cabin. She was not afraid of work and not afraid of the rough crowds she habituated. Alice carried a gun, which she knew how to use well, and had occasion to fire it. One night she was playing faro and losing. She watched the dealer and found he was cheating. She pulled her pistol on him, called him out on his cheating, took her money and left.

Alice moved to Deadwood, South Dakota, with the new boom seekers and met her second husband there. W.G. Tubbs was a gambler also and he and Alice had a strong competition for customers. They worked in the same house and were not friendly until a customer pulled a knife on Tubbs and Alice shot the man in the arm. At that point their relationship changed and the two were soon married. They set up a homestead nearly fifty miles from Sturgis, South Dakota, and gave up gambling. Alice was happy there and enjoyed their life together in the quiet, isolated place. In the winter of 1910 Tubbs caught pneumonia and died. Alice had to wait out the blizzard that had raged for several days before she could take his body to Sturgis to be buried. She had to hock her wedding ring to pay the expenses and after the burial she dealt cards to earn the money to get her ring back. She then returned to the farm but found it too lonely for her and moved to Sturgis to gamble again.

Alice began playing poker more than faro and acquired the nickname of "Poker Alice." She had taken up smoking, or rather chewing, cigars and the big black cigars became her trademark. After coming out of retirement, Poker Alice set up a place of her own where men could gamble and have female companionship afterward. She closed her place on Sundays, being a very religious person, and made the girls in her establishment attend Sunday School lessons that she taught. In her long career as a gambler, she never worked on Sundays, much to the disappointment of men she had dealt for. Alice's place in Sturgis served the soldiers of Fort Meade and Sunday closings did not stop the men from frequenting the place the other six days a week.

It was in Sturgis that she met her third husband, George Huckert. Huckert was hired to take care of a ranch Alice owned outside of Sturgis. Huckert tended the sheep and took care of the ranch and came to town when he needed supplies. He had been in love with Alice for some time and had asked her to marry him. She had refused, not wanting to marry again. After Huckert had been in her employ for some time, Alice realized she owed him for back wages to the tune of a thousand dollars. The next time he proposed, she accepted and didn't have to pay the wages. They were married only a few years before Huckert died. Alice returned to using the name of Tubbs after her third husband's death.

Her establishment in Sturgis continued to do well until one night some soldiers got very rowdy and started breaking up the place. As a last resort Alice shot one of the men who was coming at her. He died of his wound and Alice was arrested. She was found not guilty by reason of self-defense.

Not long after this incident, reformers in the town had Alice arrested for running a disorderly house. She was found guilty and convicted on this charge. Friends of Alice petitioned the governor and she was released. She closed her place and bought a small house in Sturgis. Here she tended her garden and visited with her friends until 1930. She was told she had to have a serious operation and the odds were against her, since she was in her seventies. A gambler to the last, Alice underwent the operation. This time she lost. But the memory of Alice Ivers Duffield Tubbs Huckert continues to live.

The parlor in a house of prostitution called "The Temple of Music." Courtesy of P. David Smith

25

The big fire at Cripple Creek. Courtesy: Colorado Historical Society, F-2193

Pearl DeVere

Cripple Creek, Colorado, gave legend and a final resting place to Pearl DeVere. Pearl had come from Denver when that town had begun to slow down and Pearl looked to Cripple Creek, still in full bloom, to continue seeking her fortune. She had made money in Denver and was reported to be quite wealthy. Her first house in Cripple Creek was a small one on the infamous Myers Avenue and her business prospered. She rented a horse to ride about town and no doubt cut a fine figure. Riding was a favorite sport of the ladies of leisure and it made good business sense - they dressed well, looked their best, and attracted attention.

In 1896 a fire swept through Cripple Creek, igniting the wooden buildings easily, and destroying most of the red light district. But new buildings sprang up quickly and this time a new addition to Myers Avenue had the whole town talking. The Old Homestead, as it was called, was a two story brick building with all the modern conveniences: electric lights instead of gas or kerosene, running water, two bathrooms, an intercom system and even a telephone. Heat was provided by coal stoves in the upstairs rooms and downstairs fireplaces warmed the parlors and entertainment room. The Old Homestead drew rich

A bedroom in The Old Homestead.
Courtesy: Denver Public Library Western Collection

The Old Homestead where Pearl DeVere once reigned, now a museum.
Courtesy: Denver Public Library Western Collection

clientele to its lavish rooms and the fare was the best. Fine food, excellent liquor and beautiful women were provided for those who could pay. Pearl became the proprietress of this establishment but her reign was short lived.

On a Friday night in June 1897, a party was in full swing at The Old Homestead. Rich, imported foods were served, the champagne and liquors flowed freely, and laughter swelled with the music provided by an orchestra. Pearl was dressed in a ball gown imported from Paris, made of shell pink chiffon encrusted with sequins and seed pearls and reported to have cost eight hundred dollars. The party went on until morning and then the girls retired. Pearl complained her nerves were "unstrung" and asked one of the girls to sleep with her. The house was quiet until around eleven the next morning when the girl awoke to find Pearl lying on her face, breathing heavily. She could tell something was wrong and called for a doctor. The doctor arrived and tried to save Pearl, but she had taken an overdose of morphine and could not be revived. She died that afternoon at three o'clock.

The funeral was a grand affair. Pearl DeVere's body, dressed in the exquisite ball gown, was escorted to Mt. Pisgah Cemetery by mounted policemen, the Elks Club band, and buggies filled with girls from the row. After the brief service, the band returned to town playing "There'll Be a Hot Time in the Old Town Tonight," Cripple Creek's own song. So ended the life of Pearl DeVere, but the beginning of her legend.

Ella Watson, known as Cattle Kate.
Courtesy: Denver Public Library Western Collection

Cattle Kate

The Sweetwater country of Wyoming provided a setting for the legend of Ella Watson, sometimes called Cattle Kate.

Ella was invited to join Jim Averill at his combination saloon, grocery store and post office in Sweetwater to provide feminine company for the cowhands in the area. She accepted the invitation and was welcomed in the desolate country even though she did not fulfill the image of a raving beauty. Ella had been the daughter of a well-to-do farmer in Kansas, had married at a young age, and then left her husband because of his infidelity. She had worked in several cities and towns - Dodge City, Cheyenne, Denver and Rawlins - and it was in Rawlins that she had met Jim. When Jim's cowhands continued to ask for a woman to "liven up the place," Jim decided Ella might be the girl for the job.

Ella was short and inclined to be heavy, weighing between 160 and 180 pounds. She was reported to be handy with a six-shooter and a Winchester, and equally handy with a branding iron.

In the spring of 1888, Ella brought her belongings to Averill's place and set up a one-room cabin about a mile from Jim's combination store. She also had a small corral where she kept a few head of stock. Now Jim was an enterprising man and

Jim Averill. Courtesy: Denver Public Library Western Collection

in addition to his store and Ella's place he was believed to have dealt in stolen cattle. Hard feelings had developed between the big cattle barons and the small ranchers. The Stock Growers Association had grown powerful and had passed the Maverick Bill, which made all unbranded cattle the property of the Association. Jim had written numerous letters to the Casper newspaper decrying the injustice of the big stock growers, hurling insults, and thus incurring their ire, as he became the spokesman for the small ranchers.

When Ella joined the operation, the big stockmen referred to her place as a "hog ranch." Hog ranches had started with military operations - hog raisers who supplied pork for the military post were required to set up their establishment far enough away that the smell would not reach the post. When camp followers were not allowed to stay on the post, they usually set up business at the hog ranch that then became a house of prostitution as well. Sometimes the hog ranches even included a saloon. Ella's hog ranch didn't supply pork to a military post, but she did have a few head of cattle around and she did have a good business. Cowpunchers would travel great distances for the company of a woman, and when they were running low on cash, or had none, they would bring in cattle and Ella would take them in trade. Thus came the name of Cattle Kate.

Jim would take these cattle, send them to a relay point, and then ship them to market. He also would add a few extra mavericks from time to time, using Kate's brand. Kate only had a few head in her corral at any time - too many would have looked suspicious - so the cattle were gathered at the relay point. Helping in this operation was a man named Frank Buchanan who had teamed up with Jim.

The blizzards of 1888 proved hard on cattlemen, many losing most of their herds. When spring came and the new calves arrived, Jim and Frank were out rounding up the unbranded strays and running them through Kate's corral. The big cattlemen suspected Kate's corral and began to keep an eye on it. In July of 1889, Jim and Frank were weeding out unbranded calves belonging to a large stockowner and supposedly shot the cows to keep them from following. In prosperous times the cattle owner might not have known of the missing calves or even pursued the killing of the cows, but times were not flush and Jim was not popular because of his letters to the paper. The cattle owner got word the calves were in Kate's corral and he organized a posse to take the matter into their own hands.

Kate was the first to be taken. The posse pulled up to her house and told her they were going to take her to Rawlins. She wanted to change her dress, but they wouldn't let her near the house for fear she'd get her rifle. They knew she was an expert shot. She was forced into a wagon and the party drove over to Jim's place.

Jim was also told they were going to take him to Rawlins and the men claimed they had a warrant for his arrest. He didn't see the warrant, just the rifles "persuading" him to get in the wagon with Kate. The posse drove off with the pair but a fourteen-year-old boy named Gene Crowder, who witnessed the "arrests," went off to find Frank Buchanan.

Buchanan went after the posse, which had unloaded Jim and Kate in a canyon filled with boulders and brush. He sighted the group and saw them standing near some scrub trees where they had thrown ropes over the limbs and had nooses around Jim and Kate's necks. Frank could hear some of the conversation as the men were trying to get Jim to jump off the boulder. Frank fired at the party with his pistol and they returned fire with their rifles. He was overmatched and had to retreat, so he rode for help.

The posse couldn't talk Jim into jumping from the boulder so he was pushed. Kate got the same fate shortly afterward. The drop was only a short one and not enough to break the necks of the victims, so they struggled on the end of their ropes until they choked to death. After the bodies stopped moving, the posse rode away, leaving them to hang in the sun.

Help didn't arrive from Casper until three days later. The sheriff and his posse came, cut down the bodies, and buried them. Warrants were made out and served on the men who had done the deed and a preliminary hearing was held in Rawlins a few days later. Each accused was allowed to pay $5,000 bail and they were allowed to sign one another's bail bond. The powerful cattlemen went free.

Before the trial came up in October, Frank Buchanan disappeared mysteriously, never to be seen again. Gene Crowder, the fourteen-year-old, was taken into "protective custody" by the cattlemen and died before the trial. The cause of death was said to have been Bright's disease. There was evidence he was poisoned by his "protectors."

When the trial came up, there were no witnesses to testify against the men and they were released with a verdict of not guilty. The power of the Stock Growers Association had triumphed in usurping justice.

Several months after the trial, one of the men involved in the hanging was shot and killed. No action was taken against his killer and most people felt the score had been evened somewhat.

Kate's house was purchased by one of her killers and was taken to his ranch to become an icehouse. Jim's place was torn down, the lumber used for other purposes. So the physical traces of the two were removed, but their legends remained through the years.

2000 Block of Market Street in Denver, where Verona Baldwin and Lil Lovell owned houses. Courtesy: Denver Public Library Western Collection.

Verona Baldwin

Verona Baldwin, a tall, slender girl, made her fame in California and her fortune in Denver. Verona was a cousin of the well-known "Lucky" Baldwin. Lucky owned the Baldwin Hotel in San Francisco, and speculated in land and horses. He also speculated in women, having had four wives and uncounted sweethearts. It was said that he was named defendant in more seduction and breach-of-promise suits than any other man.

At the age of twenty, Verona joined Lucky in California and taught school at his ranch. She claimed to be a member of British royalty, spoke with a cultured British accent, and always carried herself regally. Her best feature was said to have been her large, dark, hazel eyes.

Her scandal broke out and filled the papers of California and the nation from 1883 to 1887. On January 4, 1883, Verona shot Lucky through the left arm. She was arrested and jailed, even though his wound was not serious. Her story claimed that Lucky had ruined her "in body and mind." She said Lucky had assaulted her and then framed her by bringing charges of improper conduct against her and fired her from her teaching position.

The other side of the story, told by Baldwin's attorney, claimed that a servant had surprised Verona and a guest on the ranch, a doctor. The incident was reported to Lucky and he asked the doctor to leave his ranch and fired Verona. When the trial came up, Lucky would not testify against Verona and she was acquitted. After the trial Verona left California and settled in Washington territory. For three years all was quiet until Verona returned and the scandal rekindled. Verona threatened to sue Lucky for support of the child she claimed was his. Lucky hushed up the incident and Verona dropped out of sight once more.

Evidently Verona was out of the limelight as far as the newspapers were concerned, but not as far as Lucky was concerned. Sometime later she made news again when she was found insane and was committed to the state asylum at Napa, California.

In the late 1890's Verona popped up in Denver and by 1903 she had purchased the house at 2020 Market Street. She began to make her fortune and was known to be one of the most distinguished look-ing madams on the Row. She had prematurely gray hair which she wore piled atop her head with a tiara perched on top. She also wore a costume of purple velvet that enhanced her queenly looks.

Business flourished in Denver for girls of the half-world in spite of reforms by the local government. In the red light district windows were required to be covered and the girls had to stay inside rather than solicit business in the open. Many quick thinking girls punched peepholes in the curtains so that men passing would stoop and peek in, and perhaps be enticed to come inside. This practice did not occur at the finer houses like Verona's. Their clientele was more established and paid more for services. Even the finer houses, however, came under the reform on advertising their services. The signs had become so offensive to the public that after the reform took place, even the invitation "Men Taken In and Done For" was considered acceptable.

Money flowed into the house at 2020 Market Street and Verona, like the other madams, got the lion's share. The girls in the houses usually split their take fifty-fifty with the madam and also paid board out of their share. Sometimes the madams got extra cash from the dressmakers their girls patronized. All the girls had to be dressed in the latest style and look their best. Dressmakers charged high prices for their services and the madam occasionally took a kickback from the dressmaker for referring her girls to them.

As Verona's star rose, Lucky's fell. His hotel in San Francisco burned to the ground, his taxes were heavy, and he lost money. Although he still owned large tracts of land, it was undeveloped and was a burden to him.

In 1898, Lucky decided to start again. He planned to open a saloon and gambling house at Nome, Alaska, where the gold fields were booming. He left Seattle with the equipment he needed to set up business so he also took along a bevy of girls. Some reports claim he was going to open a bordello. When he arrived at Nome he could not find a suitable site for his establishment and was taken for several thousand dollars in supposed taxes. The luck that had given him his name failed him and he returned to California a few months later even deeper in debt.

Verona continued to prosper and when authorities closed down the Row in Denver, she opened a tavern called "The Baldwin Inn." She lived in a fashionable district in Denver until her death.

Girls soliciting from windows in the heart of Denver's Red Light District.
Courtesy: Denver Public Library Western Collection.

Drawing of a lady gambler playing Keno.
Courtesy: Denver Public Library Western Collection.

Madame Vestal-Belle Siddons

Madame Vestal originally came from Missouri where she had been well educated and had a fine family background, being a relative of one of the governors of Missouri. During the Civil War she had danced, attended social functions, and been escorted by young officers of the Union Army. Secrets slipped out to the beautiful young woman and she passed them on to the Confederacy. She was captured in 1862 with incriminating evidence on her person and sent to prison. Thus ended the career of the famous Belle Siddons, Civil War spy. Belle was released from prison after serving only four months of her sentence, with the promise she would not return to Missouri until the war was over.

After the war she returned to her hometown of Jefferson City, Missouri, and soon met Dr. Newton Hallett, an army surgeon from Kansas City. They were married and moved to Texas where the doctor served at an army post. The yellow fever epidemic of 1869 took the doctor's life and Belle was left to take care of herself. During her marriage to the doctor she had been taught some medicine and some gambling.

She began dealing Twenty-One in Wichita and soon had a gambling house of her own. She then changed her name to

Madame Vestal. Her business kept her moving from place to place and in 1875 and 1876 she operated a tented gambling house in Denver. As the crowds left Denver, Madame Vestal followed. Deadwood was the new Mecca, with gold drawing the seekers of wealth. New strikes of gold or silver always attracted large crowds and some of the first to move into the new areas were madams and prostitutes, looking for the free spenders who struck it rich and the "anything goes" way of life that existed in those new settlements. The gamblers were among the first to arrive also, for they could find easy money among the prospectors who found themselves wealthy overnight.

Madame Vestal took her employees, her tent and her gambling equipment with her to Deadwood. She purchased an omnibus for the journey, converted it into a comfortable, homey place and made the trip in ease with her entourage following in wagons. She changed her name in Deadwood, this time becoming Lurline Monte Verde, and set up her tent in the heart of the red light district.

It was in Deadwood that she met Archie McLaughlin, whose profession was robbing stages. Lurline fell in love with Archie and may have supplied him with information on money shipments leaving town. Archie and his gang did well until 1878, when several of the men were wounded during a holdup. Lurline went to the hideout to help one of the more seriously wounded men, who recovered and later gave evidence against the gang. The men tried a getaway to Cheyenne, but were captured. They were sent back to Deadwood to stand trial, but the stage was stopped before it reached Deadwood, and the men taken out and hanged.

Archie's death proved to be Lurline's downfall. She took up drinking, moved from place to place and died in San Francisco in an opium den.

Tents used for saloons, restaurants, boarding houses, and gambling halls. Courtesy: State Historical Society of Colorado Library.

Lil Lovell, reputed to be one of the most magnificent women of the demi-monde. Courtesy: Colorado Historical Society, Drawer b-c, Mazzulla Collection.

Lillis and Lois Lovell

Lil Lovell was reported to be one of the finest and most magnificent types of physical womanhood ever to grace the demimonde. She showed up in Leadville in 1887 and by 1889 had purchased one of the finest houses of prostitution in town. The house at 118 West 5th had belonged to Winnie Purdy, a local madam. When Winnie's business partner, a banker, found his business bankrupt, she had to sell her house. Lil's new place was decorated in Oriental luxury, with lascivious paintings adorning the walls. Velvet carpets covered the floors and rich oriental hangings and tapestries accented the finest furniture available. The house itself was a high point for visitors. Lil kept the house until 1895 and ran it well, but after Lil left, the house ceased to be a center of attention in the wide-open mining town.

Lil made her way to Denver, purchased the house at 2020 Market Street and kept it until 1903, when Verona Baldwin purchased the house.

Lil had a younger sister named Lois who joined her in the business for a short time. Lois fell desperately in love and it brought her a tragic end.

Lois met a young Denver businessman who fell in love with her and she with him. Their love continued to grow and despite

Lois' past, the young man asked her to marry him. Lois refused, knowing he had a bright future and her reputation would ruin his career. He pleaded with her; still she refused because of her love for him. The affair continued for some time, each party growing more desperate as time passed. The young man was leaving on a business trip and made a last appeal to Lois, who again said no. Feeling there was no solution to their problem, Lois made sure her lover left on his trip, then took poison and died. She was buried in the Riverside Cemetery.

The young man returned from his trip and hastened to the house to see Lois. He had done some serious thinking on his trip and had come up with a solution to their problem. They would be married, move to California and start life anew with no one knowing of their past.

When the man was told of Lois' death he was stunned. He sat in the house awhile, and then asked one of the porters to take him to the cemetery and show him the grave. The fresh grave was pointed out, the young man stood looking at it, and then he pulled out his pistol, placed it against his head, pulled the trigger and fell dead across his lover's grave.

Leadville's Ice Palace opened in 1896 after Lil moved to Denver. Laura Evens drove her sleigh into the exhibits inside.
Courtesy: Colorado Historical Society, F-2320

47

Baby Doe Tabor who captured the Silver King of Colorado.
Courtesy: Colorado Historical Society, F-20823.

Baby Doe Tabor

Elizabeth Bonduel McCourt was born in Oshkosh, Wisconsin, in 1854. She was the fourth child of fourteen in Peter McCourt's Irish Catholic family. She was nicknamed "Baby" by the family and it stayed with her throughout her life. Her home was middle class - her father was a tailor and owned a small clothing store. In her teens she was a beautiful girl who had many boys pursuing her but she set her heart on Harvey Doe, the son of a wealthy lumber dealer. Harvey was handsome, had money, was older than Baby, and his family was Protestant and Republican, the opposite of Baby's. He proposed when she was twenty years old and she accepted, much to the distress of both families. They were married in St. Peter's Roman Catholic Church after Harvey's brother, a Congregational minister, refused to marry them. The wedding was attended by members of both families and friends of the prominent Does. Harvey's father had been Mayor of Oshkosh for several terms and had a position of high standing in the social world.

After the wedding, Harvey and Baby headed for Central City, Colorado, to restart a non-working mine his father owned. They stopped in Denver on their way to Central City but were unaware that after they left Oshkosh there was a massive fire in the commercial section of town that burned both the McCourt store and Doe's lumberyard. Harvey, Sr., went to Denver and gave the couple the news that they were on their own and would have to make a living from the mine since the fire had financially strapped the Doe family and Baby's family was broke.

The couple journeyed to Central City and stayed at the Teller Hotel. Here she and Harvey explored the town's offerings. Baby wore low cut gowns in the evenings when she went out on the town and even visited the saloons and bars, which was totally unacceptable to the standards of decent womanhood. Even being accompanied by her husband did not make such behavior tolerable. Her dress and actions marked her in society's view.

Baby Doe Tabor's wedding dress. It cost the queenly sum of $7,500. Courtesy: Colorado Historical Society, F-332.

Harvey seemed to have trouble getting started on the mine and Baby stepped in and hired some men to begin working it but they ran short of money as they had spent a great deal on hotel suites both in Denver and Central City, on dining out and living a life of leisure for several months. They then moved to a small apartment over a store and Baby secured a loan from a bank for $10,000, which did not last long. The mine was not making a profit and it had to be shut down. Harvey wanted to return to Oshkosh, but his father did not want him to come back. So he found a job as a laborer in a Blackhawk, Colorado, mine and they moved to a one room apartment there. That was not for Baby and she returned to Central City and secured a job working in Jacob Sandelowsky's store. The relationship between the two raised eyebrows in Central City as Jake took her out to lunch and dinner and when Harvey returned, he took both of them out for meals. Harvey made a brief visit to Oshkosh alone and when he returned, he was ready to separate from Baby. She told him she was pregnant, so he stayed until the child was born. One writer said both Jacob and Harvey were present for the birth. The child was stillborn and Harvey packed up and moved out.

When Sandelowsky decided to move his store to Leadville, Baby followed soon after and they had adjoining rooms in the Clarendon Hotel. Silver was booming and Leadville was booming and it was a good location for a store. Some historians say that Horace Tabor, Silver King of Colorado, first saw Baby Doe when she was in Denver with her new groom and offered $1000 to Harvey to introduce him to her, which Harvey refused. Others place the first meeting of Baby Doe and Tabor in Leadville, Colorado, at the Saddle Rock Cafe. However, it was in Leadville that Tabor and Baby Doe actually met and a relationship started immediately. Tabor may have paid off Baby's debts to

Horace Tabor, Colorado's Silver King.
Courtesy: Colorado Historical Society, F-23,601.

Sandelowsky and helped secure a divorce from Harvey. Billy Bush, a long time associate of Tabor's, reportedly went to Central City and took Harvey out on the town. They went to a local house of joy and it was raided by the police shortly after their arrival. Baby filed for divorce on grounds of adultery and nonsupport and received it in a couple of weeks from a Denver judge. Horace set Baby up in a suite of rooms at the Clarendon Hotel and Baby became his mistress. Horace Austin Warner Tabor, the Silver King of Colorado, now had the best of all worlds - his wife in Denver and the most beautiful woman he knew, now his mistress, in Leadville. But Baby had a greater ambition in mind. She was determined to be his wife.

Tabor was born in Vermont in 1830. He started work on his father's farm, but became a stonecutter and met Augusta Pierce when he worked for her father in a quarry in Maine. He was twenty-seven when he married the hard working, strict Augusta. They moved west with their young son, Maxey, and tried farming in Kansas. It wasn't profitable for them and the political climate put Kansas in the middle of the upcoming Civil War. Tabor was a representative for the Kansas Territory in Topeka and knew what was coming. When the news of gold strikes in Colorado reached them, the family moved further west and Horace did some prospecting, which didn't work out. They tried several areas around Denver, and then headed into the Arkansas Valley and up to California Gulch, which became Oro City, which itself became a part of Leadville.

In Oro City, the miners stopped work and built a cabin for Augusta and Horace because ladies were so rare and revered. Horace began prospecting and they opened a store. Their enterprise worked and they made money. Augusta sold homemade bread and meals for the miners as well as keeping store. Horace became the postmaster in 1868. The area grew and expanded and Horace would grubstake some miners for a part ownership in their mines. Several of these paid off and his investments of less than $100 per grubstake returned thousands, even millions, of dollars.

In 1878, Horace was the Mayor of Leadville, and had built his family a house. As his fortune grew, he moved to Denver and built a mansion there as so many bonanza kings did. His wealth seemingly knew no end and he invested in diverse opportunities, losing great amounts of money at times and acquiring even greater amounts. He contributed heavily to the Republican Party and was interested in politics and power. He had helped plan Leadville as it grew and was very involved in banking, newspapers, railroads, and mining throughout the state. By the time he met Baby Doe, Horace Tabor was the wealthiest and one of the most powerful men in Colorado. He was the Lieutenant Governor of the state and had aspirations to become a senator.

The arrangement with Baby soon became well known but Baby tried to be discreet and wore veils when in public with Horace. They moved to Denver where he put her in a suite in the Windsor Hotel and divided his time between his mansion and the hotel. Augusta was a hard, practical, conservative woman who put down many of Tabor's ideas and Baby used that and always encouraged and flattered the man. Now he had a denigrating wife and a flattering mistress. With Baby encouraging all of his projects, he purchased and refurbished the Windsor Hotel and purchased the Broadwell Hotel and tore it down to build the Tabor Block, an expensive office building. He also began building the Tabor Opera House in Denver, an even greater and grander edifice than the one he had built in Leadville. By the time the opera house opened in September

1881, Horace had moved out of his mansion and occupied a suite in his remodeled Windsor Hotel. He sat alone in his box on the opening night of his opera house and Baby sat in the orchestra seats, gowned in turquoise satin and wearing diamonds. Baby was moved to a suite in the America House to forestall a major scandal. Augusta filed a petition for property settlement and maintenance, but not a divorce, trying to pressure Horace back into their marriage. She claimed he was worth $10 million and asked for the Denver mansion and $50,000 a year in support. Tabor listed his assets at considerably less than the $10 million, closer to $3 million.

Horace had been trying to get Augusta to divorce him, but she stubbornly refused. He sent his friend, Billy Bush, to Durango to obtain a divorce for him. The petition was filed and Horace thought it was completed, but Augusta was not notified of the action, thus making it void. Tabor and Baby went to St. Louis in September 1882 and were married in the Southern Hotel. Due to the illegal divorce, the marriage was bigamous. When a newly elected county clerk in Durango took office and started going through the records, he found the Tabor divorce on two pages that had stuck together. He also noticed that the action had not been sent to Mrs. Tabor, so he remedied that oversight. Soon after Augusta received the notice, she filed for divorce. She got the Denver mansion and $250,000 in cash. It was a very speedy divorce and was commented on in the newspapers even though many of Tabor's questionable activities did not make the papers due to his money and influence. With the divorce final, Baby threw away her veils and went out with Horace to celebrate.

In the midst of this, Horace was still pursuing his dream of being a senator and knew if his scandals came out, his chances

Elizabeth Bonduel Lillie
Tabor at the age of two.
Courtesy: Colorado
Historical Society,
F-15,354.

Rose Mary Echo Silver
Dollar Tabor at the age
of four.
Courtesy: Colorado
Historical Society,
F-5250.

would be ruined. There were two seats to be appointed, one a six year term, the other a thirty day term. With Augusta filing her divorce suit a week before the legislature made its decision on the appointee, Tabor's chances looked dim. He was passed over for the six year seat, but given the thirty day term due to his considerable support of the party over the years.

The couple set out for Washington on a chartered train a week after the appointment and set up housekeeping in a ten room suite at the Willard Hotel. Baby planned an official wedding and Horace was sworn in as Senator from Colorado. Invitations were sent to all members of the Senate and to President Chester Arthur. Baby's family from Oshkosh - her mother, father, two brothers and a sister attended. Tabor's son Maxey did attend although he and his father had a strained relationship, presumably over the divorce. The wedding of March 1, 1883, was held in the ballroom of the Willard Hotel at 9 p.m. and conducted by a priest who didn't know both parties were divorced and evidently saw no problem with the twenty-four-year age difference. Baby wore a white satin gown costing $7,500, which featured a very low neckline. Horace gave her a $75,000 diamond necklace as a wedding gift. She danced with the President while her family watched. Baby had achieved her goal even though many of the wives of senators did not attend the lavish event.

The Senator and his bride returned to Colorado after he had served his thirty-day term and moved into a house on Welton Street. There were rumors of Horace continuing his political career, and even running for President, but those dreams died when Baby had Horace install her brother, Peter McCourt, as manager of the Tabor Opera House. Billy Bush, Tabor's long time associate, had been doing the job and liked it very much but was fired to make room for Peter. So Bush sued Tabor and Tabor countersued, with both suits being dropped, but the resulting disclosures of Billy's activities for Tabor ended Tabor's political career.

Baby became pregnant late in 1883, and she turned her thoughts to her upcoming motherhood. On July 13, 1884, their first child was born and named Elizabeth Bonduel Lillie Tabor. Baby decided to have a party for Lillie when she was a month old and sent out one hundred invitations. Only two accepted. Denver society had shut Baby out and would not budge for all of Horace's millions. The same group openly embraced Augusta, the wronged and respectable wife. So Baby accepted the verdict and entertained Horace's friends and business acquaintances but made no more plans for mixed social events or parties.

In 1886 Tabor purchased an estate on Sherman Street, in the Capitol Hill district of Denver. Even though it was one of the finest houses in the city, he had it remodeled to Baby's specifications. Baby was denied nothing - she had servants, Paris gowns, diamonds and the finest carriages, even peacocks strutting in the yard. She attended the opera, this time sitting in the silk-lined Tabor box, and drew as much attention as the performers on stage. On October 17, 1888, Baby gave birth to a son, Horace Joseph Tabor, but he died the next day.

The Tabor empire was showing some signs of financial difficulty but as one mine would falter, another ore strike would come along and bail him out. Slowly, however, the production was dropping and a day of reckoning was coming.

In December 17, 1889, Rose Mary Echo Silver Dollar Tabor was born. She, as well as her sister Lillie, were beautiful children and grew to become beautiful women. Lillie was blond like Baby, but a quiet, stubborn child. Silver Dollar had dark hair, but her mother's merry disposition.

In 1892, a financial panic struck the nation. Men lost their jobs, banks failed and the national debt rose. As this crisis continued, President Cleveland persuaded his party to repeal the Sherman Silver Purchase Act in 1893, and Colorado and its silver mines were doomed. The price of silver dropped from $1.33 an ounce to forty-seven cents an ounce. It was a deathblow to Tabor and his holdings. He had borrowed against his real estate to keep the mines in operation. All of his properties except the Matchless Mine in Leadville were foreclosed on. He and Baby were now poor. They moved to the Windsor Hotel when their Sherman Street house was taken, but were only there a few days before it, too, was foreclosed. From there they moved into a cottage in a poor section of the city that rented for $25 a month. Some writers say Tabor returned to Leadville and took a job pushing wheelbarrows of slag for $3 a day. Others say he purchased a home near Ward, Colorado, and began mining for gold. Baby and the girls stayed in Denver, living on the edge of poverty.

When a friend of Tabor's, Winfield Stratton, heard of the plight, he went to visit the Tabors. After seeing their situation first hand, he visited with a senator to get Horace appointed postmaster in Denver. After all, Tabor had donated the land for the post office and over the years had contributed vast amounts of money to the Republican Party, and he had been a postmaster before. So he was appointed to the vacant post on January 1, 1898. He had a salary of $3,500 a year - a far cry from the $100,000 or more a month he was accustomed to, but it was enough to provide for his family. Baby stuck with him through the years of poverty, much to the surprise of everyone in Denver and those elsewhere who knew the circumstances of their relationship. Baby was only in her thirties and still a beautiful woman. She could have moved on if she wanted. Horace worked for the post office for a year and three months.

His appendix ruptured and he declined to have the surgery that might have saved him. Peritonitis set in and Horace lived seven days before losing his battle to the infection. Baby was at his side day and night. Legend says he repeatedly told her to "hold on to the Matchless; when silver comes back it will make millions." Duane Smith, in his Tabor biography, says there was no evidence to support that. Tabor was buried at Mount Calvary Cemetery in Denver in 1899.

After Horace's death Baby had offers for marriage and other arrangements but she turned them down and moved to Leadville with her two daughters. She evidently had strong ties to the town as she had made numerous visits there during her marriage. She lived in rooming houses with the girls and tried to raise money to get the Matchless going. Lillie was sixteen and hated everything about her life. She wrote letters to her McCourt grandmother complaining about their situation until her Uncle Peter sent her the money for a train ticket to Oshkosh. She packed and left and Baby Doe never saw her eldest daughter again. Silver liked Leadville and adjusted better to their changed circumstances. But she also left when she was twenty-one and died accidentally in Chicago at the age of thirty-six.

After the girls were gone, Baby moved into a shack next to the Matchless Mine. Over the years she would get money to do some digging in the mine and was bailed out of mortgages on the property by former friends of Horace. But the mine did not produce and Baby became a haunted-looking creature who drew attention by her odd assortment of castoff clothing. She charged her meager supplies of food - stale bread and such - at the local mercantile store and the county paid the bill out of their charity fund.

In February 1935 Baby purchased her groceries as usual and headed back to the mine in the beginnings of a blizzard. It snowed heavily for two weeks and after the storm broke, a neighbor noticed there was no smoke coming from the chimney on Baby's shack. She got help from a nearby prospector and they dug a path through the drifts to the place. There they found Baby stretched out on the floor, cold as ice. Some reports said she froze to death in her newspaper-lined cabin. Others believe she had a heart attack.

Baby spent years as a lonely, lost woman, clinging to the Matchless Mine. She lost her riches, her looks, her husband, and her children; yet she continued to try to mine the Matchless. If penance on earth is possible, one suspects Baby Doe had paid hers in full.

Her funeral was arranged and paid for by one of her brothers, Phil McCourt. She was buried in Denver with hundreds, including the social women who shut her out, attending the service. Her legend lives on in books and an opera.

Etta and Sundance Kid in the "Wedding Photo" taken in New York.
Used with permission of Pinkerton, Inc.

Etta Place

The most mysterious woman of the old West would have to be Etta Place. Beautiful, refined, well dressed, educated: one look said "respectable." Yet she lived, off and on, with Harry Longabaugh, called the Sundance Kid, and his associate, George Leroy Parker, better known as Butch Cassidy. Both men, along with their gang, the Wild Bunch, were wanted by the law for train and bank robberies as well as a few murders. She may have participated in some of their robberies - certainly a few bank robberies in South America, and perhaps a train or two.

Her beginnings are not really known. Some say she was the granddaughter of an Earl, attended a teacher's college, and taught school for a short time, some say in Denver, some say in Telluride. Others believed she worked in a Texas house of prostitution. Even the Pinkerton Detective Agency was unable to trace her beginnings or her real name. She came to the public's attention and was placed in legend by the movie "Butch Cassidy and the Sundance Kid."

Most of Etta's activities were documented by the Pinkertons in their pursuit of Butch, Sundance and the Wild Bunch. It's believed Etta was born around 1874 and went to Robber's Roost in 1896.

The lonely, desolate area on the Colorado-Utah border was a favorite hideout for the gang. Etta was the second woman in the camp; the first was the wife of Elzy Lay, a member of the gang. She described Etta as a very beautiful woman with a perfect complexion, masses of dark hair and a stately figure. Etta left the camp in the spring after staying a few months and her activities are unknown until she left Texas with Sundance and started on the journey that would lead to South America.

The gang had gone to Texas and was staying there when they had their photo taken. It seems several of them had been roughhousing and had destroyed each other's hats, so they went to town and purchased new derbies and suits to go with them. They decided to have a photo made in their new finery. Inadvertently, it would lead to their downfall. The photographer kept the negative and put a copy in his window for display. A Wells Fargo agent saw the photo, recognized Will Carver, and sent copies to law officers and the Pinkertons, who identified the members, one by one, and then used the photo to make wanted posters.

Sundance and Etta left Texas and went to Pennsylvania to visit his family on their way to New York where they would join up with Butch. The trio had decided to move to South America. Etta was introduced as Harry's (Sundance's) wife to his brother and sisters and plans of their upcoming move and new life were no doubt discussed. From there the couple went to Buffalo, New York, to check into Dr. Pierce's Invalids' Hotel. The private hospital was an expensive place and was frequented by three presidents among others. It's believed Sundance was treated for an old bullet wound in the leg and an infection in his nose and throat. Etta also checked in and her treatment was speculated to be for venereal disease or something related to her appendix, a recurring problem for her. Hospital records listed Etta as twenty-three or twenty-four years old, five feet five in height, and weighing one hundred ten pounds. The records said she had gray or blue eyes and medium dark hair. After release from the hospital, the couple spent a few days at nearby Niagara Falls, a popular honeymoon spot. Then it was on to New York City and their meeting with Butch. Although Etta played the role of Harry's wife, no marriage record has yet been found.

It was February 1901 when the threesome rented a second floor suite in a boarding house on West Twelfth Street. Butch posed as Etta's brother and Sundance was introduced as her husband. The quarters had windows facing the street, always a necessity for Butch and Sundance. They stayed there about three weeks. While in town, they saw the sights, ate in fine restaurants, took in the theater and did some shopping. It was here that Etta and Sundance had their photo made that is usually called the "wedding photo." Etta is dressed in velvet and Sundance wore formal tails. Their photo was also used to make wanted posters later. But the twosome would be in Argentina before any of the posters came out - not only the one of Etta and Sundance but the one of the Wild Bunch as well.

For whatever reason, Butch did not go with the young couple to South America, but returned to Montana and staged another train robbery. Etta and Sundance, using the name of Mr. and Mrs. Harry A. Place, boarded the S.S. Herminius on February 20, 1901, headed for Argentina. They arrived in Buenos Aires in late March and stayed at the Hotel Europa, still using the name "Place," which was Harry's mother's maiden name. Sundance deposited the equivalent of $12,000 in the London & River Plate Bank and they embarked on a tour of the region, looking for a suitable spot for a ranch. After several months of scouting they settled on a place in western Patagonia close to the Andes. The land was suitable for cattle and the country had no extradition treaty with the United

The photo that put the Wild Bunch on "Wanted" posters. The Sundance Kid is sitting at the left end and Butch Cassidy is

States, which made it attractive to people who found themselves on the wrong side of the law. The appearance of the country in South America also reminded North American westerners of the land in the United States and drew a number of Americans because of that. The ranch was in the Cholila Valley and was four square leagues in size. It was located one hundred fifty miles from the coast of Chile, just over the mountains, and sixteen hundred miles from Buenos Aires. They planned to raise cattle and sheep and drive them over the mountains into Chile and to sell them there at a good profit.

Butch joined the couple a year after their arrival and the two men made application to settle the land. Butch used the name Santiago Ryan from 1901 to 1905 and Etta and Sundance continued to use the name Place. The ranch was stocked with 300 cattle, 1500 sheep, 28 saddle horses and some chickens. Shortly after Butch joined them, Etta and Harry made a trip to the United States in May of 1902. They stayed three months and checked into a hospital for more treatment, visited Coney Island and spent some time with Harry's brother and sisters. Butch wrote letters to friends and family telling of his loneliness. The couple returned to Buenos Aires on a freighter, the Honorius. Before going back to the ranch, they rested at the Hotel Europa and closed their account at the London & River Plate Bank. It contained $1,105.50. From Buenos Aires they took a steamer and then pack mules to reach the ranch.

The trio had built a cabin similar to ones found in the American West. It had planked walls, four-pane, double-hung windows, burgundy and gold wallpaper, a cast iron stove, brass lamps and later, a telephone that connected to a lookout building 200 meters down the road. There was even a small secret room under the floor in the cabin. And they had some hired hands to run the ranch. The threesome entertained visitors and used china and linens like "proper" people. They rode their horses daily, participated in roping the cattle and prospered on their ranch. Etta, always the fashion plate, wore pants and boots and was described as a "good rider and an expert with a revolver." The group mixed well with native Argentineans as well as foreigners, though Butch seemed to be the most gregarious and the best liked. Sundance was quiet as was Etta, but her beauty always drew notice.

In 1904 Etta and Harry returned for a visit to the States. This time they went to the World's Fair and Exposition in St. Louis and also visited Ft. Worth, Texas. It was in 1904 that a Pinkerton detective discovered the trio was living in Argentina. He wanted to go after them at the ranch but was told by a neighbor that it would be impossible during the rainy season (which was not true). So he returned home and notified the agency of his findings. The Pinkertons wanted to mount a full scale search but the bankers and railroad associations who had financed a great deal of the search for the Wild Bunch were not interested in footing the bill for an Argentina expedition. They felt as long as Butch and Sundance were out of the United States, they wouldn't be robbing their banks or trains. But the Pinkertons had distributed posters and information on the threesome to South American police and the territorial governor had ordered their capture. There was a $10,000 reward posted on them. That made life much more precarious as anyone could turn them in.

In 1905 the trio got word that detectives were in the country looking for them. They gave away their furniture to neighbors and hid out for about a year. They were credited with robbing a bank in Rios Gallegos, which netted around $100,000. In December of 1905, another bank was robbed in Villa Mercedes and there were four Americans in the group, one of whom was probably Etta. They were pursued by a posse and ended up shooting one of the horses of the followers as the group escaped across the mountains into Chile. Several reports said the group rode through torrential rains to escape their posse and even took a raft across the Salado River, stole some horses and headed into Chile.

Butch and Sundance made their way to Bolivia and Etta disappeared from the scene. It was reported she was taken to Denver in 1906 or 1907 for an appendectomy. Others said she was pregnant. After this time, Etta's trail is obscure. No one knows her actual fate. Butch and Sundance took jobs working for the Concordia Mines in Bolivia. There they met Percy Seibert, an engineer with the company. Seibert's recollections contributed much to what is known about Butch and Sundance's experiences in South America. Butch and Sundance were good hands for the company and Seibert became good friends with Butch. He knew some of their past and that they were robbers with a price on their heads, but he liked and respected them. Seibert was told by Butch that Etta was the best housekeeper in the Pampas, but a whore at heart. Seibert found Butch to be congenial, a "good fellow," and Seibert respected his good deeds - he had stopped a kidnap attempt of another mine owner by warning him of it and had, on another occasion, ridden two days on a mule to warn a Concordia official he was an assassination target. Butch even confessed to Seibert he decided not to rob a certain mine because the owners had been so nice to him. And when an employee reported the pair was going to rob the Concordia, Butch said they didn't rob the people they worked for. But in time, Butch and Sundance went back to robbing banks.

The shootout at San Vicente on November 6, 1908, was most likely the end of the two outlaws, even though many sources claim they were not the ones who died there. Their end, and Etta's, may forever be clouded in mystery. But their story will continue to fascinate readers of Western history.

Mattie Silks in her forties.
Courtesy: Colorado Historical Society, F-32-942.

Mattie Silks

Mattie Silks (Martha A. Silks) of Denver was a madam at the age of nineteen in 1865 and bragged "she had never been a prostitute and never worked for another Madame," according to Ronald Dean Miller in *Shady Ladies of the West*. Mattie began her "career" in Springfield, Illinois, and moved to Olathe, Kansas, where she was run out of town by the conservative citizens. She then moved to Kansas City. She ran houses in Dodge City, Abilene and Hays City in the summers when the cattle drivers were in town and spent the winters in Kansas City. As the cattle towns settled down, Mattie moved to Georgetown, Colorado.

Golden haired Mattie ran a brothel on Brownell Street in Georgetown. Here she made the fortune that allowed her to launch her Denver operation. And here she met Cortese D. Thompson, known as Cort, who played a prominent role throughout most of her life and who would spend a large amount of the fortune she made. Cort's occupation was being a professional foot racer, which was a very popular sporting event in every town in the West until the turn of the century. Each town had its favorite runner, usually a member of the local fire department, and this man would run against a professional like Cort. Naturally, there was heavy betting on such events and sometimes the races were fixed. Cort was a handsome man - nearly six feet tall with sandy hair, a light colored moustache and a lean build. He hailed from Texas and thought of himself as a Southern gentleman who was above work of the regular sort. He also gambled constantly, lost frequently, drank heavily, and was extremely attractive to women.

In 1876, Mattie left Georgetown for the wide open city of Denver. She was twenty-nine years old. Cort moved with Mattie and they lived together as they could not marry due to a wife in Texas who would not give Cort a divorce.

Mattie first rented a house on McGaa Street, but soon purchased 501 McGaa and hired twelve "boarders" to occupy the house. McGaa Street had a series of name changes. It became Holladay Street, named after Ben Holladay (a transportation mogul in Denver), because he fell out of favor with the citizens there. In 1889, Holladay's heirs petitioned the Denver aldermen to change the name again and they did, this time to Market Street. Mattie purchased several buildings on the street and rented them to other madams.

Mattie fought a pistol duel with another woman - perhaps the only formal duel of its kind. The duel took place in Olympic Gardens in Denver. Mattie had thrown a champagne party for the "ladies" of the row to celebrate a race Cort had won and that she had won a thousand dollars betting on. The other duelist was Katie Fulton, another madam. The cause was Cort. It seems Katie had been trying to lure Cort away from Mattie for several weeks and the situation came to a head at the party. Seconds were appointed - Cort was Mattie's and a gambler was Katie's. They stepped off their thirty paces beside the Platte River, turned and fired. Mattie's bullet lodged in a tree, but Katie's struck Cort in the neck. Mattie attended him and when she couldn't stop the bleeding, put him in a hack and took him to

Denver General Hospital. Cort survived the ordeal but the question of whether Katie shot him accidentally or intentionally was never answered.

Life was good to Mattie and she prospered in spite of bailing Cort out of gambling debts and buying expensive clothes and buying racehorses. She would go to Kansas City to purchase clothes and to get away from her recognition in Denver. She was known as the Queen of the Red Light District and was easily recognizable due to her likeness to Lily Langtry, the leading actress of the time. And the blue eyed Mattie did everything she could to emphasize the similarities. Mattie's dresses were expensive, though not necessarily tasteful, and all had two pockets - the left held gold coins and the right pocket housed her ivory handled pistol. She claimed Wild Bill Hickok had taught her to fire a pistol when she was in Abilene and he was town marshal.

In 1881, Mattie leased the house at 527 Market Street (called Holladay at the time) to Jennie Rogers, who later would rival Mattie for the title of Queen of the Underworld. However while Mattie reigned she spent a great deal of time at Overland Park attending the races and watching her horses run. Unfortunately, her losses were greater than her winnings, but she continued her racing activities and held on to her stables.

Cort received word in 1884 that his wife had died so now he was legally free to marry Mattie. Since Cort owed her around $50,000 that he had borrowed over the years to cover his gambling debts, it behooved him to marry her. This they did on July 6, 1884, and the wedding was performed in Peru, Indiana, only a few hundred miles from Springfield, Illinois, where Mattie started her career. Perhaps Peru was her hometown or she had relatives there that made her choose that location. After the wedding they honeymooned at Niagara Falls.

During the mid-eighties, the City of Denver was courting the St. Louis Railroad to come to Denver. When the president of the railroad came to town he was given the keys to the city and to Mattie's house. He was quite smitten with Mattie and invited her on a month-long journey in his private railroad car. She refused but later gave in to pressure from the Chamber of Commerce and even Cort. So she went to California on the private car and posed as the man's wife as they mixed with the social elite. She must have enjoyed playing the role of a respectable lady as the tour lasted two months instead of one. The deal for the city fell through, however, and the railroad did not move to Denver. Mattie had a good time and the Chamber paid a $5000 bank note she owed to show their gratitude for her services.

In 1886, Cort was notified that he had an orphaned granddaughter. His daughter had died and left Cort the only relative as her husband had abandoned her. Cort didn't feel obligated to care for the child but Mattie did. She knew that many of the women who turned to prostitution had come from orphanages. So she had Cort purchase a ranch near Wray, Colorado, some distance out of Denver, and she put up the money. The ranch served several purposes for Mattie. She could move her horses there, she could have Cort look after the operation and keep him away from the gambling houses, and maybe she could quell the rumors he was seeing a prostitute named Lillie Dab.

Cort purchased some cattle and hired a few cowpunchers to look after them and the wife of one of the men looked after the child, named Rita. Soon Cort acquired a reputation for running off other people's cattle and altering their brands to his. When Mattie went out to check on the operation she fired the foreman and hired a new one named Handsome Jack Ready.

Cort continued his swaggering ways and when he visited

Denver he became bolder in his visits to Lillie Dab and didn't try to cover them. Mattie heard the stories and didn't believe them for a while. But in March of 1891, she caught the two of them together and shot at Lillie, taking off one of her curls. Lillie fled the room, and later town. Cort grabbed the gun from Mattie before she could shoot him and he beat her severely. Mattie filed for divorce the next day and got a restraining order that Cort could not sell the ranch or anything on it since she had paid for everything. This evidently brought Cort to a realization that he would be destitute without Mattie. So he begged her forgiveness and deeded the ranch to her. She took him back and dismissed the divorce suit eleven days later.

When Queen Victoria's Diamond Jubilee Celebration took place in 1897, Mattie and Cort announced to the Denver underworld that they were going to attend and make it a second honeymoon. Mattie still held her position as Queen of the Demimonde and the trip, though expensive, was a reminder to her community of her standing. When they returned from their junket, Denver was virtually deserted. The gamblers and red light district inhabitants had left for the Alaska gold rush to fleece the men flooding there in search of their fortunes. So Mattie and Cort and several of her "girls" loaded up and headed to Dawson City.

Prices in the Yukon were high. In addition to the trip expenses, Mattie paid $400 a month for a rented house and $50 a month for protection money. They spent three months in the rain and mud of the Yukon before Mattie decided to return to Denver. Cort had developed a very bad cold that didn't respond to treatment. Since pneumonia was a serious and prevalent disease, Mattie wanted to leave before winter set in and they would be locked in until spring. The trip was extremely profitable - only three months had netted Mattie $38,000.

She reopened her house at 1922 Market Street and resumed business. Cort's cold improved in the dry Denver air and he returned to the ranch at Wray but left the running of it to Handsome Jack Ready who had taken care of it during his absence.

Life proceeded as usual for a couple of years until April of 1900. Cort went to Denver to get $5000 from Mattie to buy more cattle. She refused, but did give him $1500. Several days later she heard that he had gambled and drunk away the money and had to borrow money to get back to the ranch. Mattie was afraid he might sell her favorite horse so she wired the sheriff at Wray to arrest and hold him until she could get there. When she arrived she found Cort in terrible pain. A doctor was called and said it was stomach cramps. He gave Mattie laudanum to administer to ease Cort's pain. She nursed him through the night, but he died by morning. The doctor ruled his death one of ptomaine poisoning. One writer suggests it was more likely caused by cirrhosis of the liver, as Cort had been a heavy drinker for most of his life. Mattie paid for his funeral and his burial plot in Fairmount Cemetery.

With Cort gone, Mattie adopted his grandchild Rita, who was without a legal guardian. The girl was nearly sixteen years old at the time and married at the age of eighteen. After Rita's marriage Mattie sold the ranch and moved Handsome Jack Ready to Denver. There he worked as a bookkeeper and a bouncer for her. He was big enough and strong enough to take care of anyone who got out of line.

When Jennie Rogers, a rival leading madam, died and her estate was finally settled, Mattie purchased her house at 1942 Market Street for $14,000. She had her name - M. SILKS - inlaid at the front door in white tile. That acquisition gave her three houses on Market Street- numbers 1916, 1922 and 1942.

Mattie's standing as Queen of the Row was coming to an end as prostitution was abolished in Denver in 1915. With that property values dropped and there was no way to keep the money coming in. She tried running a hotel for a while - the Silks Hotel - but gave it up. She kept a few of her things, sold the rest of her furnishings at auction and moved to a cottage on Lawrence Street. At the age of seventy-seven Mattie fell and broke her hip. She married Handsome Jack Ready to have a caretaker and left her estate to him and Cort's granddaughter. Mattie died in 1929, at the age of eighty-three. When her estate was settled and all the bills were paid there was only $1,922 remaining. Mattie had made over a million dollars in her lifetime. She was buried at Fairmount Cemetery under the name Martha A. Ready. Next to her was an unmarked grave that held Cortese Thompson.

The parlor of mirrors after Jennie and Mattie had ceased business.
Courtesy: Colorado Historical Society, F-36,403.

Jennie Rogers, a leading madam in Denver.
Courtesy: Colorado Historical Society, F-37,953.

Jennie Rogers

Jennie Rogers (legal name Leah J. Fries) arrived in Denver in 1880. She had worked in Pittsburgh and St. Louis, where she ran a high-class house of prostitution. When she reached Denver she leased a house at 527 Holladay from Mattie Silks. Jennie later purchased the house for $4,600. She was a dark haired, lovely woman with an air of elegance and was reputed to have a quick and ready wit. As Jennie prospered, she and Mattie became rivals for the dubious honor of "Queen of the Row."

The house received a renovation under Jennie's management. She had it papered and painted from top to bottom and replaced all the furnishings to put her signature on it. After the house was purchased she bought the adjoining house and added it to the first by knocking out walls. Soon after that project was completed she purchased a third house. Jennie added bars to the windows so she could open the windows and air the house of stale smells of tobacco, perfume and alcohol. Most of the bordellos kept their windows closed and shades drawn. The bars had an added benefit of preventing the women in the house from allowing their favorite men to enter the house without paying.

Jennie was seen on any pleasant day riding in a two-wheel trap, pulled by a matched pair of horses. She dressed modestly and drove through the wealthier neighborhoods of Denver. Even though she might look like a respectable lady when she ventured out, she was recognized in the community.

It was rumored Jennie had a boyfriend from St. Louis who visited her every month or so. He was supposedly the Chief of Police in that city and it is said she hung an oil portrait of him in the Holladay Street house. He figured as the lead in a story attributed to Jennie of how she acquired her next house - the house at 1942 Market Street known as the House of Faces and Mirrors.

The story involves a wealthy Denver businessman who wanted to run for the office of governor. He had started his career working for another businessman, took over the business, later married the man's wife and prospered in the booming economy. But his first wife had mysteriously disappeared before he married the second. There had been no hint of foul play or any suspicious actions until the man made his political move. Then people began to ask about the disappearance and if he had gotten rid of her in order to marry the second wife and improve his social standing. Jennie's boyfriend is credited with capitalizing on the rumors by setting up a blackmail scheme. He obtained a skull from an above-ground Indian burial, buried it in the back yard of the wealthy man, then called at the gentleman's house with a bogus search warrant. He represented himself as a member of the District Attorney's office and had his "investigators" dig up the skull. He then made a deal with the man to forget the charges if he would give Jennie $17,000. And that is how Jennie supposedly acquired the money to finance her finest house, one that surpassed Mattie's.

The large gray stone house rivaled houses in San Francisco and was certainly the most opulent of all the Denver houses. On the front were five carved faces - at the top of the third floor was the face of a woman, no doubt representing Jennie. Then along the top of the second floor were the faces of two men and two women. Many have said these represent the political hopeful who paid for the house, his two wives, and Jennie's boyfriend. There were other carvings on the facade - one of a horseshoe in a bed of lotus leaves and phallic symbols along the first floor front.

Inside, Jennie had bird's eye maple tables with mother-of-pearl inlay, oriental rugs, paintings, plush furniture and two grand pianos. There was a parlor of mirrors and in the ballroom a sixteen-foot circular mirror on the ceiling. When the house opened, Jennie, elegantly gowned, and her twenty girls waited for the "guests" beneath crystal chandeliers in the parlor of mirrors. The entryway had a walnut staircase that led to the rooms above and painted cattails adorned the walls.

After completing this project, Jennie leased the house next door, cut an adjoining door between them and furnished that residence in the style of a Turkish harem.

Jennie's boyfriend dropped out of the picture soon after her new house was completed and she married a bartender from the Brown Palace Hotel and set him up in his own business. The marriage lasted until she caught him with another woman. She shot and wounded him, and then filed for and received a divorce.

As Denver grew and became more respectable the city fathers yielded to pressure from the community and passed an ordinance that all the prostitutes should wear yellow ribbons in their hair when they were out shopping in town. This way the decent women could avoid them on the street. Jennie and

Mattie got together and organized an unusual retaliation. On the day after the ordinance passed, all of Denver's prostitutes paraded on 15th Street wearing yellow ribbons in their hair and yellow stockings, yellow shoes, yellow dresses and carrying yellow parasols. After that the ordinance was ignored.

Jennie also played a humanitarian role during the Panic of 1893, by supporting a hundred destitute girls. They were respectable women who had come to Jennie for work when they lost their office and retail jobs but she would not hire them and did not allow the other madams to hire them either. She put them in respectable boarding houses until she could send them home.

In 1904, Jennie married Archie Fitzgerald. He was from Chicago, supposedly a politician, and they married in Arkansas. They only had a few years together as Jennie died in October 1909, of Bright's Disease. Archie and some out of state relatives inherited her estate. After the estate was settled, Archie sold the Market Street house to Mattie Silks.

After Jennie's death, Mattie had her name spelled in tile on the doorstep of the House of Faces and Mirrors. Courtesy: Colorado Historical Society, F-32-942.

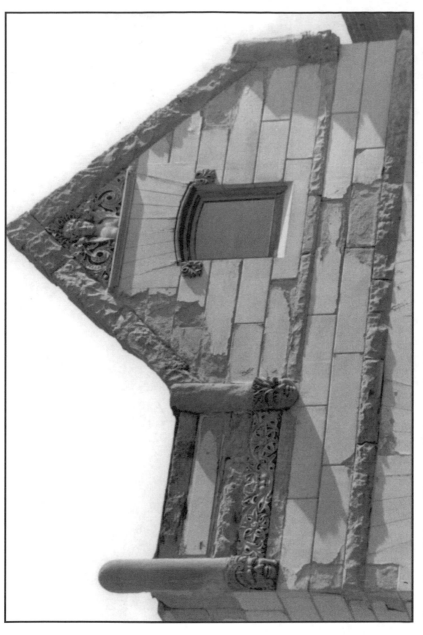

Jennie Rogers' House of Faces and Mirrors. Jennie's face in the peak and three of the four faces carved below her image. Courtesy: Colorado Historical Society, F-25,190.

Laura Evens dressed as a nun for a charity masquerade in Central City.
Courtesy: Colorado Historical Society, Mazzulla Collection.

Laura Evens

Laura Evens* was born in 1874, supposedly in the deep South and to a wealthy and influential family. She claimed to have attended a convent school in Missouri for awhile. She married at seventeen but evidently did not care for domestic life and turned to prostitution. She began her life in the demimonde in St. Louis, but like so many others in her profession, the excitement further west prompted her to move on. She worked in one of the houses on Market Street in Denver, and then headed to the boomtown of Leadville. There she worked as a dance hall girl and prostitute and even filled in as a clerk for Augusta Tabor at the Tabor store. She supposedly got into trouble with Augusta for cutting beefsteaks three times thicker than they should have been.

In the early days of Leadville there were so few women in the camp that all women, even prostitutes, were treated with respect. Men standing in long lines at the post office to collect mail would fall back when any woman entered to allow her to go first in line. By the time Laura arrived in Leadville, there were many changes, even a ban on prostitutes promenading on Harrison Avenue, the main street. Laura was an outgoing, fun-loving person who was "a

Laura's name is seen spelled Evans in many places, but her tombstone reads Evens.

talented vocalist, an accomplished dancer, brilliant conversationalist, and an inveterate card player," according to Fred Mazzulla in *Brass Checks and Red Lights*. She also liked to drink a lot and was always game for an escapade. While in Leadville she had several adventures that made the town take notice of her. When the circus came to visit, she noticed the Roman chariots drawn by horses and decided a chariot ride would be an exciting adventure. She bribed the caretakers at the circus to let her use it and tore around town, even down Harrison Avenue, at breakneck speed, scattering pedestrians and animals. The excitement came to an end when she lost a wheel turning a corner and was pitched into the dirt street. Laura was not injured, nor did she learn a lesson from the event.

When Leadville opened the Ice Palace in January 1896, Laura borrowed a sleigh and a horse named Broken Tail Charlie and rode past the hitching post and past the ice statue of Lady Leadville and straight into the palace. Inside, the horse and sleigh ran into some exhibits, damaging them. Broken Tail Charley became overexcited, kicked the sleigh and broke it. He then broke loose and headed back to his stable.

Laura was known to be honest and was called upon to help break a mining strike at the Maid of Erin Mine. Since the area was surrounded by a heavily armed guard of union sympathizers, no one could go in or out. The owner needed to get payroll to his superintendent at the mine and asked Laura if she could do it. She said yes. She took the money and put it under her skirt and rode sidesaddle up to the mine. When stopped by the guard, she gave him a story about needing to visit a dear friend who was working there. The guard let her through and the strike was broken. The owner gave Laura $100, had her to dinner at his house in Denver and took her to a party in Denver where he introduced her as his secretary.

Laura liked to defy the "respectable" world. On a visit to a friend in Central City, she donned a nun's outfit and went to a charity masquerade. She even had her photograph made in the nun's clothing to prove she had done it.

She left Leadville near the end of 1896 and moved to Salida. Laura liked the "good life" - lots of money, clothes and parties. She worked on the line for four years and then purchased her own house, where she had the best of furnishings, clothes and girls. The house was furnished with velvet drapes and plush sofas and her girls wore silk garters with ten dollar gold pieces on them. She purchased a row of cribs across the street to increase her revenue and became an economic force in the town. Since Salida was a major railroad town, she had a lot of railroad customers.

In 1918 a flu epidemic struck the community and Laura and her girls helped nurse the sick, cooking and caring for them. When the epidemic ended, the girls returned to business in the Front Street house. Several years later the town decided the landmark must be closed. So Laura turned the house into a rooming house for railroad men and put a sign on her door that said "No Girls." When crime increased in the town, Laura was asked to reopen her house. She refused, saying she was happy with her railroad boarders and they were settled in.

In April of 1953, Laura died; some say the last of the famous madams. She was buried in the local cemetery with a simple headstone and in a lavender colored casket. To the end she remained in good physical shape, played cards and rolled her own cigarettes.

Probably an early day Leadville "house." Courtesy: Denver Public Library Western Collection.

Mollie May

Mollie May reigned as one of the top madams of Leadville from 1879 to 1887. Leadville was in full swing with silver pouring out of the surrounding mountains and millionaires being made daily. Entertainment abounded in Leadville - gambling halls were open continuously with dealers working eight-hour shifts before being relieved. After the shift was over many dealers visited other gambling halls to play for their own pockets. Theaters provided various amusements in the bustling city. Each evening a brass band congregated in front of each theater on State Street and played for an hour or so, each trying to outdo the other, then proceeded to parade through the town to draw business for their particular theater. Small boys carried banners announcing the night's fare, be it can-can dancers, a play, tumblers and acrobats or female bathers. The bands then returned to State Street and played in front of the theaters until the performance began at nine o'clock. In addition to the gambling halls and theaters, one could find amusement in the dance halls, beer halls, saloons and brothels.

Leadville had a population of 30,000 at one point and a reputation of being one of the toughest towns in the nation.

Harrison Avenue in Leadville, the main street. Courtesy: Denver Public Library Western Collection.

Men were robbed on the street nightly, homes were broken into while the occupants were there, and murder was commonplace. French Row, Coon Row, Tiger Alley, and Stillborn Alley nurtured vice of every description. Three opium dens were located near French Row and men disappeared into the area, never to be heard from again. Stillborn Alley got its name from the number of babies found dead there and the reports of small babies found in garbage heaps were accepted as normal.

A newcomer to Leadville and recent law graduate from Princeton, George Elder, wrote home to his family of the dance hall area, "I seldom go down that street but when I do I always notice them full and lots of music and noise. The women are the most forlorn pieces of humanity I have ever seen. One of them down at the 'Red Light' committed suicide last night by taking poison.... It does not make any difference how many of them die, there seems to be a perfect scramble to fill their places."

In the midst of this wide-open town were the madams and their girls. In 1879 Mollie had a fine house at 144 Main Street (also known as West Third Street). It was a large house that even had a telephone - one of the first in Leadville. She sold this house to the city for $10,000 and they used it for the City Hall offices. Mollie's former house of prostitution provided offices for the mayor, city clerk, city council, and the police. In 1880, Mollie acquired title to 129 and 131 West Fifth Street, where the other fashionable madams resided. In her new location she had neighbors like Frankie Paige, Carrie Linnel, Winnie Purdy and Mollie Price, all brothel owners. And at 133 West Fifth, next door to Mollie, was Sallie Purple's house.

Sallie and Mollie got into an argument around midnight one night, supposedly a dispute over the merits of Connaught and Tipperary as birthplaces. The two women barricaded themselves

State Street in Leadville. Courtesy: State Historical Society of Colorado Library.

in their houses and fired rounds of ammunition at each other. The girls and guests in both houses joined in the fray, pumping lead into the houses. After an hour or so, the firing stopped and the paper reported the participants were "resting on their arms and awaiting daybreak to resume hostilities." Tempers evidently cooled in the waiting process and business went on as usual. Miraculously no one was hurt.

Mollie's name showed up in the paper for the ordinary reasons - occasionally one of her girls would take poison to end her tragic life in the brothel or to end her suffering over a man who "did her wrong." Usually the girl was discovered before it was too late and was saved to live through another love affair. Young girls of thirteen and fourteen would run away from home and seek admittance in the houses. They were taken in and the police had a constant effort to find the girls and pull them away from a life of sin.

In September of 1880 the police raided Mollie and three other madams. The city derived money for their coffers by fining from $25 to $100 a month, depending on the class of patronage the house received. The madam and the girls were expected to pay. Some had been delinquent in their payments and the city needed money. Seventeen girls were arrested in the raid and the Leadville Daily Herald reported two "nice young men" leaped from the second floor of Mollie's house while the raid was in progress, to escape being taken in and having their names in the paper. The Carbonate Weekly Chronicle said of the raid, "There is weeping of glass eyes, gnashing of false teeth and tearing of mohair switches in four of the gilded, not to say the brass mounted palaces of sin of Leadville today." The houses raided were Mollie's and her neighbors', Sallie Purple, Frankie Paige on West Fourth Street and Carrie Linnell on Second Street. Each "lady" was required to pay $25 to show for trial. The women had some unkind words to say to the officers and the judge. The newspaper reported wrote that a policeman told him there was another reason for the raid. "The force [police], he said, were not on the best of terms with the Aldermen, on account of delinquent salaries, and they had information last evening that several members of the august body might be found at some of the palaces pulled, and that the license business was only a blind." The reporter covered his reputation by writing, "The *Chronicle* don't [sic] pretend to give this as a fact, for it believes that all the Aldermen are too good and modest and virtuous to do such a thing, but the statement was repeatedly made, and it was claimed it could be readily substantiated." The girls paid their fines, were released, and went back to business.

In April and May of 1882 Mollie again made headlines - this time with a baby scandal. Word got out that Mollie was buying a nine-month-old baby girl from a Mr. and Mrs. Moore. Members of the press and local citizens raised some serious doubt as to Mollie's motives for the child. On April 30, Mollie released a notice to the *Herald* that the parents of the child were not Mr. and Mrs. Moore and that "if anyone attempts to interfere with the little one, the real mother will make herself known and show that it is not a subject for public comment." This was an attempt to throw off some of the criticism she had been receiving. On May 11, Mollie gave an exclusive interview to the *Herald* because they had treated her fairly and kindly in their reports. Mollie told them she was adopting the baby until the mother, who was a decent but very poor woman, could contact her mother, tell her of the marriage and birth of the child, and receive assistance. Then the real mother would adopt the child, Ella, from Mollie. Mollie showed her anger with the insults and insinuations she had received by telling the reporter she had never refused any charities and had regularly donated to churches and hospitals.

On June 6 of the same year Mollie made the papers once more, this time with a less serious situation. Mollie had a warrant issued for Annie Layton for stealing a dress from her. Annie, in turn, issued a warrant on Mollie for running a house of ill fame. Mollie retaliated with a warrant that Annie was an inmate of a house of ill fame. The reporter summed up the situation by saying, "It is likely these charges will be withdrawn, as both parties would be almost unable to prove their charges without criminating themselves." On June 7 the charges were dropped for want of prosecution.

Mollie remained in the background until her death in 1887. According to the *Leadville Carbonate Weekly Chronicle*, Mollie died shortly after 8 a.m. on Monday, April 11, from neuralgia of the heart. Her illness lasted only a few hours before her unexpected and untimely death.

The *Chronicle* stated Mollie was originally from Illinois and left her home after giving herself to a "lustful suitor." She started her wayward career of prostitute and dance hall performer in the West and drifted from place to place until the early 1870's when she began performing in Cheyenne at Jim McDaniels' theater. Her "fresh figure and features" were said to be very popular with the audience of cowboys and freighters. In 1876 Mollie moved to the Black Hills (coincidentally, Jim McDaniels began a theater operation there as well).

The *Chronicle* said, "Here she seized the scepter from her rivals and began to reign as their queen. Scores worshipped at her shrine, the successful suitor being Jim May, one of the leading freighters over the Black Hills road, and a brother of the notorious Boone May." Jim enjoyed her favors until he found he had a rival - his brother Boone. Jim and Boone and Mollie met in the Gem Theater and had an altercation that resulted in Boone firing a pistol to kill his brother, but struck Mollie instead. Boone was disarmed by the crowd and Mollie was taken out of the auditorium of the theater to a nearby cabin. She was stunned, but not wounded as the bullet hit the steel in her corset and glanced off, thus saving her life. Whether this is a story Mollie told on herself or whether the reporter had heard it and attributed it to Mollie, it's doubtful the story is true. An extremely similar incident did take place in Deadwood, but Estelline Bennett wrote in *Old Deadwood Days* that "Lou Desmond shot a girl who had stolen her lover from her, but the bullet glanced off the heavy steel of the lady's...corset and saved her life." It's doubtful Mollie was the girl Lou Desmond shot, but Mollie may have borrowed the story and changed it to suit herself.

The *Chronicle* also related that Mollie was missing a portion of one ear, which was bitten off by Fanny Garretson in a dispute over Jim Brown. Fanny was a singer and had taken a fancy to Jim, who was a banjoist. The three were in a closed carriage when the argument broke out and Mollie lost a piece of her ear. This, too, would have taken place in Deadwood.

According to the *Chronicle* Mollie arrived in Leadville in 1878 and remained there until her death nine years later. McDaniels had made plans to open a theater in Leadville and shipped 40,000 pounds of scenery and property there in January 1879. One has to assume a connection of some kind between McDaniels' move and Mollie's move. McDaniels did open a theater there and ran it for several years before moving to Denver.

Two articles in the *Carbonate Weekly Chronicle* of April 18, 1887, described Mollie's funeral and the funeral oration. The funeral took place in her residence (brothel) at 129 West Fifth Street. Gathered there was a large crowd of madams and prostitutes and men from the community. The Reverend Prentiss delivered the service over an open coffin at 2:30 in the afternoon on Wednesday, April 13. He asked the mourners to gather around and recited two of the Psalms and a long extract from 1 Corinthians, Chapter 15. Then he began his eulogy:

"Friends - As Mark Anthony said to the Roman people over the dead body of the assassinated Caesar, 'I come not to praise, but to bury Caesar.' So, to the people of the community I say, 'I come not to praise, but to bury. To my order it is especially offensive, as I know it must be to all right thinking people, to have the character of a friend dissected in public. Indeed we are accustomed to regard it to expose personal character in public, as it would be to expose a nude body. This much would I say:

Speak kindly of the erring, and do not thou forget,
However deeply stained with sin, he is thy brother yet.
Heir of the selfsame heritage, child of the selfsame God,
He has stumbled in the path thou hast in mercy trod."

Reverend Prentiss continued with the story of Jesus in the Jewish temple confronting sinners and the prostitute and telling them he did not condemn them but to go and sin no more. He spoke of those who were ostracized by society and society's view of them and quoted the scripture, "Let him that is without sin among you cast the first stone." He reminded the gathered crowd of the certainty of death and the uncertainty of its advent, and that each person would have to account for his actions on Judgment Day. The Reverend said to those who were burdened by sin and truly penitent and longed for peace and pardon, go and sin no more. The crowd wept profusely.

After the service the coffin, which was very costly for the time period, was placed in the hearse to be taken to the cemetery. This hearse was brand new and had taken a first premium in New Orleans at an exposition of funeral products. It was said to be one of the finest in the country and cost $3000. There were two carriages in the procession costing $1,300 each and they made their public debut on this trip. There were six carriages rented by the estate and the turnout was said to be one of the largest in the city. The coffin was completely covered with flowers sent by the surviving "sisters." All accompanied the remains to Evergreen cemetery where Mollie was buried at the age of thirty-nine.

The *Leadville Evening Chronicle* of April 11, 1887 noted Mollie's death in an article entitled, "Last of a Noted Landlady" and gave a maiden name of Milinda May Bryant, the daughter of Thomas and Bessie Bryant. On the same page was a Funeral Notice for Miss Jennie Mickey, another name Mollie used. The 1880 census shows Mollie coming from Virginia and lists her as Mollie May. It also shows she had ten "boarders" - all listed as prostitutes, even two men who lived there. Her household ranged in age from twenty years old to thirty-four years old.

Bills submitted for Mollie's final arrangements included $150 for the casket, rental of the hearse, $10, and rent of six carriages for $36. Her cemetery plot expenses were $40. The estate showed personal property sold for $1,500 and her house was sold to Anna Ferguson for $3,600 cash.

Mollie's estate was handled by J. H. Monheimer and it was surmised most would go to her adopted daughter, now approximately six years old, and in school in the East. Court records indicate the child was called Ella Moore and was attending St. Scholastica's Institute in Highland, Illinois. Her guardian was listed as Robert Buck. The *Chronicle* said, "It was always known that the foster mother idolized the child and that her life was wrapped up in its future." An article in the June 24, 1901 *Herald* stated that a pretty blond named Lillian Moore, who was just twenty years old and "reputed to be the adopted daughter of Mollie May, who years ago was the queen of the women of the half world of Leadville," had attempted suicide a week before. She went to a room at 414 Pine Street, the home of "Will Allen, colored," was jealous of him and drank a solution of cocaine. Two doctors were called to the scene, pumped her stomach and saved her life. She took a train to Denver. That is all that is known of Mollie's adopted daughter.

The town had admired Mollie, in spite of her occupation. Her eulogy written by Frank Vaughn, of the *Herald Democrat,* took the form of a poem. It is even more significant today as Mollie's grave in Evergreen Cemetery is devoid of any gravestone or marker, yet there is a large evergreen tree growing on her plot.

Mollie May

Think of her mournfully,
Sadly, not scornfully -
What she has been is nothing to you.
No one should weep for her,
Now there is sleep for her -
Under the evergreens, daisies and dew.

Talk if you will of her,
But speak not ill of her -
The sins of the living are not of the dead.
Remember her charity,
Forget all disparity;
Let her judges be they whom she sheltered and fed.

Keep her impurity
In dark obscurity,
Only remember the good she has done.
She to the dregs has quaffed
All of life's bitter draught -
Who knows what crown her kindness has won?

Though she has been denied,
The tears of a little child
May wash from the record much of her sin;
Whilst others weep and wait
Outside of Heaven's gate,
Angels may come to her and lead her in.

When at the judgment throne,
The master claims his own,
Dividing the bad from the good and the true.
There pure and spotless,
Her rank shall not be less
Than will be given, perhaps, to you.

Then do not sneer at her,
Or scornfully jeer at her -
Death came to her, and will come to you.
Will there be scoffing or weeping,
When, like her, you are sleeping
Under the evergreens, daisies and dew?

Mollie May lies buried under the evergreen. Author's collection.

Bibliography

Books

Beebe, Lucius. *The American West.* New York: E. P. Dutton & Co., 1955.

Bennet, Estelline. *Old Deadwood Days.* New York: Charles Scribner's Sons, 1935.

Best, Hillyer. *Julia Bulette and Other Red Light Ladies.* Sparks, Nevada: Western Printing & Publishing Co., 1959.

Blair, Edward. *Leadville: Colorado's Magic City.* Boulder, Colorado: Pruett Publishing Company, 1980.

Brown, Dee. *The Gentle Tamers.* New York: G. P. Putnam's Sons, 1958.

Drago, Gail. *Etta Place: Her Life and Times with Butch Cassidy and the Sundance Kid.* Plano, Texas: Republic of Texas Press, 1996.

Drago, Harry Sinclair. *Notorious Ladies of the Frontier.* New York: Dodd, Mead & Co., 1969.

Eberhart, Perry. *Guide to the Colorado Ghost Towns and Mining Camps.* Chicago: Sage Books, 1959.

Ellis, Amanda. *The Strange, Uncertain Years.* (An Informal Account of Life in Six Colorado Communities) Hamden, Conn.: The Shoe String Press, Inc., 1959.

Emrich, Duncan. *It's an Old Wild West Custom.* New York: Vanguard Press, 1949.

Feitz, Leland. *Myers Avenue.* (A Quick History of Cripple Creek's Red-Light District) Denver: The Golden Bell Press, 1967.

Griswold, Don L., and Griswold, Jean Harvey. *The Carbonate Camp Called Leadville.* Denver: The University of Denver Press, 1951.

Horan, James D. *Desperate Women.* New York: G. P. Putnam's Sons, 1952.

Horan, James D, and Sann, Paul. *Pictorial History of the Wild West.* New York: Crown Publishers, Inc., 1954.

Hunt, Inez, and Draper, Wanetta W. *To Colorado's Restless Ghosts.* Denver: Sage Books, 1960.

Kimball, Nell, *Her Life as an American Madam by Herself.* New York: The Macmillan Co.,1970.

Mazzulla, Fred and Jo. *Brass Checks and Red Lights.* Denver, Colo., 1966.

Miller, Ronald Dean. *Shady Ladies of the West.* Los Angeles: Westernlore Press, 1964.

Mumey, Nolie. *Poker Alice.* (Alice Ivers, Duffield, Tubbs, Huckert {1851-1930} History of a Woman Gambler in the West) Denver: Artcraft Press, 1951.

Parkhill, Forbes. *The Wildest of the West.* New York: Henry Holt & Co., 1951.

Redford, Robert. *The Outlaw Trail.* New York: Grosset & Dunlap, 1976.

Ross, Nancy Wilson. *Westward the Women.* New York: Alfred A. Knopf, 1944.

Smith, Duane A. *Horace Tabor, His Life and Legend.* Niwot, Co.: University Press of Colorado, 1989.

The Women. (The Old West; v.23) The Editors of Time-Life Books with text by Joan Swallow Reiter. Alexandria, Virginia: Time-Life Books, 1978.

Williams, Brad. *Legendary Women of the West.* New York: David Mckay Company, 1978.

Willison, George F. *Here They Dug the Gold.* New York: A. L. Burt Company, 1931.

Articles
Irey, Eugene. "Leadville's Inglorious Miltons," *The Colorado Quarterly* (Boulder, Colorado), Vol. I, No. 2 (Autumn, 1952), pp. 211-223.

Unpublished Material
Sanford, Albert B. "Silver Heels." State Historical Society of Colorado, Denver, Colorado.

Other Sources
Leadville newspapers, 1870-1901.

Leadville City Directories, 1879-1901.

U.S. Census Records 1880.

Index